James Date's

EXMOOR
& *WEST*
SOMERSET

James Date's
EXMOOR
& WEST
SOMERSET

COMPILED BY HILARY BINDING AND W.H. (BEN) NORMAN
WITH AN INTRODUCTION BY PROFESSOR JOHN HANNAVY

EXMOOR BOOKS

First published in 2002 by Exmoor Books
Image Copyright © 2002 Lyddon Family Archive
Textual Copyright © 2002 Hilary Binding, W.H. (Ben) Norman
and Professor John Hannavy

ISBN 0 86183 471 2

British Library Cataloguing-in-Publication-Data
A CIP data for this book is available from the British Library

EXMOOR BOOKS
Official publisher to Exmoor National Park Authority
Exmoor Books is a partnership between
Exmoor National Park Authority and Halsgrove

Halsgrove House
Lower Moor Way
Tiverton EX16 6SS
T: 01884 243242
F: 01884 243325
E: sales@halsgrove.com
www.halsgrove.com

Printed and bound in Great Britain by
Bookcraft Ltd, Midsomer Norton

❧ CONTENTS ❧

Watchet when the railway terminus for this branch of the Bristol and Exeter railway, c.1871. A Gooch locomotive is being turned around on the turntable ready for the return trip to Taunton on the broad-gauge line. In the background is the first harbour crane bought by Thomas Griffiths in 1870.

INTRODUCTION

James Date and Photography

by Professor John Hannavy

Photography was less than twenty years old when James Date acquired his first camera. As far as can be ascertained, he had no formal training in the new art, and yet almost immediately he started taking pictures which showed immense technical understanding, and considerable compositional talent. Initially engaging with photography as a hobby, he later turned professional, but seems always to have retained his passion and his enthusiasm for the medium, continuing to take photographs for his own and his family's enjoyment, as well as for his growing clientele.

According to local trade directories, there was a 'James Date, Grocer & Draper' in Watchet as early as 1840, and there is a strong likelihood that it was the same man, by this time living at Myrtle House in Swain Street, who turned his hobby into his profession and opened a glass-house studio in the late 1850s or early 1860s.

James Date was a remarkable photographer, but by no means unique. He was just one of thousands of talented men and women throughout the country who turned to the new art of photography in the 1850s and 1860s, and through whose cameras we catch a fleeting glimpse of times long past. His enthusiasm for recording both the important and trivial details of his time and his place, and his abilities at capturing that elusive animated sense of activity in his pictures – so difficult with slow plates and cumbersome cameras – are what makes him remarkable. In other towns in other parts of the country, there must have been countless other James Dates who are still waiting to be celebrated. Their images are our most tangible links with Victoria's Britain, and because they wrote its story from a 'local' and 'everyday' point of view, they perhaps told it more completely than the famous and celebrated names from photography's past century and a half.

Date was equally at home on location or in his studios in Watchet and Dunster, and his business acumen was obviously considerable. He fused his meticulous approach to the technical aspects of his photography with a great eye for a picture, and an ability to turn the ordinary into a sometimes wry observation on life. His wonderful studio ambrotype of the butcher selling a rack of mutton to the local hotel owner is a case in point.

While Victorian photographers were often commissioned to photograph their subjects in their working environments – albeit reconstructed in the studio – images like that suggest a real fascination with human interactions.

His studio would have looked like a large greenhouse, the glass roof draped with calico blinds which could be opened or closed to control the amount of light falling on the subject. The expanse of

A hand-tinted quarter plate studio ambrotype depicting Henry Chidgey, landlord of the London Inn, purchasing a rack of mutton from Mr Thorne, the local butcher.

(COURTESY OF BEN NORMAN)

glass walls, a glass roof, and an assortment of giant reflector screens meant that photography – by daylight of course – could be carried on throughout the working day. The studio would, almost certainly, have been north-facing, as direct sunlight created harsh and unflattering shadows. A series of white reflector screens to direct light into the shadows and black velvet or calico screens to cut out direct sunlight could be adjusted to suit the conditions, ensuring that the light which fell on the subject remained ideal as the sun moved around the sky.

With long exposures necessary – especially on dull days – Date's studio would have been equipped with a range of what looked like instruments of torture, but were in fact clamps to hold his subjects in place. Concealed behind crinolines or long coats, and behind tables, the adjustable stands could hold a head in place, offer a comfortable rest for a raised arm, or keep a recalcitrant child from moving. With

portrait photography an expensive indulgence – which could so easily be spoiled by movement – studio subjects were happy to be subjected to such indignities.

And contrary to the widely held belief, Victorians looked stern in their portraits not because they were without humour. Quite simply, it was considered inappropriate for the respectable British to smile for the camera. In any case, holding a smile and not blinking were almost impossible with exposures ranging from several seconds to a minute or more, and with a clamp digging into the back of the sitter's head.

As the majority of portraits would be trimmed to fit the popular carte-de-visite format, little care was taken over the studio clutter which might be included in the untrimmed picture. Thus the remarkable tea party and other group photographs which Date left us untrimmed give a wonderful account of his studio and its layout.

In this studio portrait of Date with family members – which the photographer would perhaps have eventually trimmed to fit the carte-de-visite format had it been for a commercial portraiture client – reflector screens can be seen leaning against the wall. The photographer would have used these to bounce light back into the shadow areas of the picture.

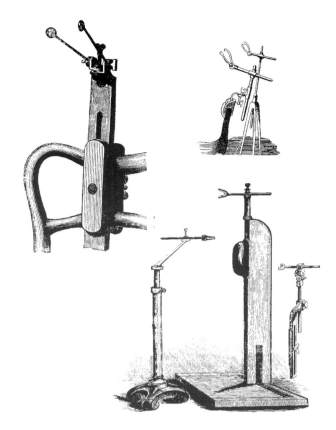

Studio portraits in the 1860s were seldom large, and in a small town such as Watchet, perhaps only rarely so. In small provincial towns, the demand was predominantly for smaller and less expensive portraits. A photographer like Date, mixing studio photography with location, needed different instruments for the different demands of outdoor and indoor work. We know he had at least four cameras.

As it was not normal to enlarge photographs in those days, the final image size dictated the size of camera used to take the picture. The most common portrait sizes were quarter plate (107mm x 83mm), sixth plate (83mm x 70mm), and the ubiquitous carte-de-visite (95mm x 60mm). Quite often, one camera could be adapted to all three of these formats, simply changing the size of the plate holder at the back, and perhaps changing the focal length of the lens.

The cameras seen in the portrait of James Date suggest three formats. To his left is a quarter plate sliding box camera of late 1850s design, and this might also have been used for both sixth plate and carte-de-visite. Behind him is a large bellows field

To keep subjects still during the long exposure in his glass-house studio, Date would have used restraints like these. Photography in the 1860s was expensive and, if the subject moved, probably painful as well!
(JOHN HANNAVY PICTURE COLLECTION)

James Date and his cameras. A sixth plate albumen print from wet collodion negative. Images so far identified confirm that Date used at least four formats — sixth plate, carte-de-visite, quarter plate and half plate. Images from the largest camera shown in this picture have not yet been identified.

camera, probably taking 10" x 8" negatives, while to his right is a lightweight field camera, taking 'whole plate' (165mm x 215mm) or 'half plate' negatives (165mm x 105mm). His fourth camera, of course, was used to take the portrait itself. It was a sixth plate instrument, probably of a design which had been in common use in studios since the early days of the daguerreotype and the ambrotype. Quarter plate, sixth plate and ninth plate ambrotypes by James Date survive in the Watchet Museum.

Photography in Date's day was a particularly cumbersome procedure. The days of mass production of either equipment or materials were still decades in the future. The photographer in mid-Victorian times had to be technician, artist, chemist and innovator. Cameras were large and heavy, and as exposures were relatively long, a heavy sturdy tripod was needed to keep the camera steady. Not for James Date was there the luxury of travelling light and working quickly. While today's photographer can buy 35mm film in any corner shop or supermarket and have it processed just about anywhere, Date and his contemporaries had to manufacture their own materials as well as take the pictures, and then process them themselves. While today's photographers can shoot a roll of 36 exposures in a matter of a few seconds, a photographer on location in the 1850s and 1860s had done a good day's work if eight or ten successful negatives resulted from that effort!

Although the medium was still very young by the time James Date acquired his first camera, it had undergone several considerable advancements since Louis Daguerre in France and Henry Fox Talbot in England in the late 1830s had independently invented two quite distinctive and different ways of making photographic images. The French daguerreotype, announced in 1839, produced a unique direct positive image on a silvered metal plate, while Talbot's calotype – patented in 1841 and evolved from his earlier 'photogenic drawing' process of 1835 – generated paper negatives from which any number of positive prints could be made.

Neither of these two pioneer processes was still in vogue when Date turned his attention to photography. They had both been superseded by what became known as the wet collodion process introduced in 1851 by the Englishman Frederick Scott Archer. Archer's process used a glass plate coated with a volatile mixture of guncotton, ether, and potassium iodide, and dipped in a silver nitrate sensitising bath to create a light-sensitive coating. The ether evaporated quickly, and if the collodion

was allowed to dry, the mixture became relatively insensitive to light. In its tacky state, however, it offered photographers a reliable and versatile process capable of producing very high quality negatives after relatively short exposures. This was the process James Date took up, probably in the late 1850s – a likely starting date given the accomplishment of his photography by the very early 1860s.

The wet collodion process could be used in two ways. The more common was the production of high quality glass negatives, from which any number of prints could be made, much as we do today. The alternative approach was to under-expose and then slightly under-develop the negative, allowing only a thin ghostly image to appear. That was then fixed and either laid on black velvet or backed with a black shellac varnish. The result was a unique positive image known in Britain at the time simply as a collodion positive, but now widely referred to using the American term of ambrotype. We know from surviving examples of James Date's work that he was equally accomplished at either variant of the process. At Watchet Harbour he produced both ambrotypes and negatives, and several fine ambrotypes survive from his Watchet studio. The majority of his images are, of course, paper prints from collodion negatives.

His negatives were all printed on albumen paper, the standard photographic printing paper of the day, and one of the first photographic materials to be at least partially mass-produced.

While the collodion process offered the photographer exposures that were shorter than ever before, the necessity of using the process wet introduced other hurdles which had to be overcome. Working in a studio, it was no problem preparing the plate in an adjacent darkroom just before exposure, and developing it immediately afterwards, but on location, even just a few yards from the studio, that requirement brought with it some considerable logistical challenges. Not only did the photographer need to carry his camera, tripod, and lenses, he also had to take some sort of portable darkroom, and all the materials and chemicals necessary to prepare, coat, sensitise and subsequently develop and fix the negatives.

By the time of the earliest pictures illustrated in this book, the collodion process had been around for ten years and a whole range of innovative answers to the portable darkroom problem had been designed and marketed. From large horse-drawn darkrooms that could double as living accommodation, down to ultra-lightweight dark tents, there was a solution to fit every photographer's need. Perhaps James Date even knew Mr Heineken of Sidmouth, who in 1859 published details of the lightest portable dark tent yet put on the market – claiming that as it was so lightweight, it enabled its users to reach the parts other photographers could not reach!

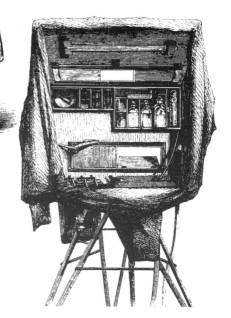

The collodion photographer had to take a portable darkroom with him wherever he went, in which he would coat his plates before exposure and develop them afterwards.

(JOHN HANNAVY PICTURE COLLECTION)

Most photographers had more than one portable darkroom or dark tent. If they were working with large format cameras, they may have used a more robust carriage-based approach, while if they were working with a small camera, a collapsible dark tent – that could be transported as a backpack – would often suffice.

We know from surviving examples of Date's work, and from the portraits of him in his studio, that he used at least four different camera sizes. The largest, used for his commercial output, appears to have taken negatives about 10" x 8" in size, while the smallest camera, designed originally for stereoscopic or 3D photography, took two images each about 70mm x 62mm on plates approximately 84mm x 140mm. This is a somewhat eccentric size, as most Victorian stereo cameras used a wider plate – approximately 84mm x 170mm – and may suggest that Date used a bespoke camera of a more compact design than normal. The same camera, fitted with an alternative holder for sixth plate size negatives, may also have been used for the majority of the remarkable illustrations in this book. We know from the main body of the album from which these images originate, that the prints thus produced were trimmed down to 55mm x 65mm.

Stereoscopic photography was one of the medium's first widespread enthusiasms. The principles behind it were quite simple – two pictures were taken from two camera positions the same distance apart as the human eyes. When the resulting images were viewed through a special stereo viewer, the brain reassembled the scene with the full 3D sense of depth and space that can be appreciated with normal human vision.

Many camera designs incorporated two lenses, and the two exposures were taken simultaneously. Date's camera, however, had a single lens on a sliding lens panel, and the two component images were taken one after the other. That made the camera lighter and probably cheaper, but had a major drawback. Unless everyone in the scene stood perfectly still for the duration of not one but both exposures, their image might appear in two different places on the two plates. When seen through the viewer, they would therefore appear as ghostly figures in two separate locations within the image. Such anomalies are evident in several examples of Date's stereoscopic ambrotypes, taken during the rebuilding of Watchet Harbour after the great storm in 1861, and during the construction of the West Somerset Railway in the same year.

Another surprising anomaly is the fact that the images are laterally transposed in the final stereo pairs. When an image is created in a camera, it is inverted and laterally transposed by the lens. So, the left-hand image, when turned round to read the right way up, becomes the right-hand image. With a negative from which prints were made, you simply transposed the prints. But with the ambrotype – where the final image was the actual plate that was in the camera – the normal way round the problem was to coat the back of the glass with black shellac, and look at the image emulsion side up. To protect the emulsion, a cover glass was usually placed over the

Identified as No.1 in what must have been an extensive series of images, and dated 7/61, this stereoscopic ambrotype is captioned 'From the Old Pier Head, Watchett (sic!). It probably shows ore from the Brendon Hills about to be loaded onto a waiting ship.

(JOHN HANNAVY PICTURE COLLECTION)

Un-numbered and undated, and captioned only as 'Watchet Harbour', this stereoscopic ambrotype looks across the rebuilding work to the busy harbour, seen here at low tide. Only at low tide would the ships remain static during the long exposure. Beyond can be seen the 'far-famed Alabaster Cliffs' as Date described them in his advertisements, early 1860s.

(JOHN HANNAVY PICTURE COLLECTION)

delicate image, the two plates then being bound together with passe partout tape. Date took a simpler approach, placing a card covered with black shellac against the emulsion side of the camera plate, and binding the two together. The result is that the right-hand image is where the left should be and vice versa. This produced a strange effect when seen through a stereo viewer, quite different from that seen with paper prints. Did he not understand the

optical laws that govern stereo vision – that the left eye should read the left image and the right eye the right image? Apparently not!

As a commercial photographer, James Date was alert to the potential of the growing tourist market in West Somerset, and appears to have decided very early on in his professional career to exploit it fully. If the surviving examples of his work are representative of his output generally, he had an eye for the sort

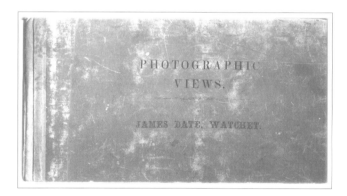

JAMES DATE,
PHOTOGRAPHIC ARTIST,
WATCHET,
Has just received a large supply of STEREOSCOPES, at prices varying from 10d. to 27s. 6d.—Also a quantity of SLIDES, from 4d. upwards. — Sedgfield's new American and English Scenery, 1s. each.
☞ Views taken for the Stereoscope.

James Date acted as a sales outlet for other photographers as well as selling his own work. Russell Sedgfield was a highly successful landscape and architectural photographer whose stereoscopic views were sold throughout the West of England, Wales and the Midlands. This advertisement comes from the first edition of the West Somerset Free Press *ever printed, 28 July 1860.*

(COURTESY MAURICE AND JOYCE CHIDGEY)

of images his customers would wish to buy and take home with them. His views fall into three general sizes, the smallest of which would undoubtedly have fitted the carte-de-visite format. By the mid-1860s, the scenic carte was widely bought by holiday-makers and visitors throughout Britain. Included in Date's catalogue were many views of Watchet's historic harbour, Dunster and the other charming villages along the north Somerset coast, and local churches and stately homes. The same locations were photographed in the larger quarter plate size and also in the smaller sixth plate. Small albums of

views (*see below*), sometimes assembled to the customer's individual requirements and tastes with the images pasted onto 245mm x 130mm pages, were bound in distinctive blue covers bearing the legend 'Photographic Views, James Date, Watchet'.

For his many retail outlets, Date assembled albums of views containing eight, twelve, sixteen or twenty-four images, either quarter plate or carte-de-visite size prints. They were priced at 2s., 3s., 4s. or 5s. respectively, while albums of the larger 'cabinet' sized prints could be purchased at an additional charge. The prints were described as 'printed on good toned paper', as even in those early days of

photography, there was a growing understanding that un-toned prints were more likely to fade than toned ones. Gold toning, the most effective method, has ensured that many of these fascinating images have survived for over one hundred and forty years in remarkable condition.

Date also produced *The Handbook of Watchet and Neighbourhood* which could be purchased in 1867 'with photographic illustration' for the princely sum of 8d. in what he described as 'the cheap edition'! Hard-bound, and with eight albumen view prints pasted in by hand, the 'Best Edition' cost 2s.8d. A bespoke version of the handbook could be assembled with the customer's own choice of photographic views, suggesting that Date might have supplied his retail outlets with loose prints as well as fully assembled books and albums. He also offered loose prints for sale 'unmounted, at a reduced price, for pasting in scrap books'.

Both the handbook and the albums were sold through a number of local booksellers and stationers including A.K. Baldwin in Watchet, Mr Slater in Dunster, Mr Cox in Williton, Mr Barnicott in Taunton and Mr Newton in Minehead.

In addition to the books and loose prints, the booksellers also offered 'a variety of photographic views of Watchet and neighbourhood for Album and Stereoscope, including the far-famed Alabaster Rocks, &c., &c.' In the late 1860s Date also offered 'seven new views on note-paper' – a reference, which may refer to hand-made prints on a thicker, matt finish alternative to the shiny-surfaced albumen printing paper. Despite the familiarity of the subjects – including Watchet Harbour from the Pleasure Grounds, the Brendon Hill Incline and the delightfully misnamed 'Washford Abbey' of which many other views have survived – so far, none of these prints has been identified.

This book, and the images which follow, serve as an introduction to James Date, and his personal view of Victorian Somerset. Much additional research needs to be done to establish a fuller understanding of his photography and how he came into the profession. Was he self taught – or who might have introduced him to the 'black art'? Was he successful? So many early photographers had more than one string to their bow – styling themselves 'photographer and bookseller', 'photographer and innkeeper' and a host of other unlikely combinations. But James Date, with his main premises in Watchet and a second glass-house studio in Dunster 'which place he visits every Friday (weather permitting)' seems to have found a formula which worked – meeting the photographic portraiture needs of the local community as well as the tourist needs of the visitors. It was a combination that other photographers throughout the land also tried to turn into a successful business. James Date's legacy to us is contained within these pages. Through his lens we see his family, his studio and his neighbourhood as it existed in a bygone age, when photography was the technological miracle of the age, and when the photographer was considered little short of an alchemist. James Date's magic still speaks to us today.

Taken at the eastern end of the Esplanade, this fascinating view shows the cable system used to deliver buckets of mortar to the masons working on rebuilding the harbour. Stereoscopic, simply captioned '57. 9/61 Watchet Pier'.

(JOHN HANNAVY PICTURE COLLECTION)

Building the West Somerset Railway

(JOHN HANNAVY PICTURE COLLECTION)

A group of family or friends sit beneath the famous cliffs. Half of a stereoscopic ambrotype, 1860s.

(JOHN HANNAVY PICTURE COLLECTION)

Identified as No.3, 7/61, and captioned 'From the old Pier Head, Watchett (sic!), this stereoscopic ambrotype uses the masts of the ship in the foreground to create an additional sense of depth.

(JOHN HANNAVY PICTURE COLLECTION)

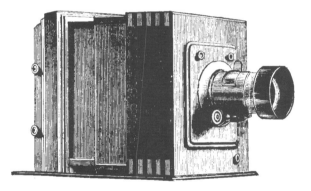

Studio Camera
This deisgin of camera used wooden box sections which slid inside each other. Heavy but very stable, they were used on heavy studio tripods.

(JOHN HANNAVY PICTURE COLLECTION)

Field Camera
The lightweight bellows camera reduced the weight which had to be carried out on location. After use the camera would be folded flat and carried in a backpack or carrying case.

(JOHN HANNAVY PICTURE COLLECTION)

∽ FAMILY PICTURES ∾

James Date was born in 1807 and married Elizabeth Stoate (b.1812) when they were both very young. They had four sons between 1828 and 1840: James, Richard Stoate, John Stoate and Edwin. Ann was born in 1845 and Mary in 1847. The family lived at Myrtle House in Swain Street – now the house next to the Town Council Offices – and it is probable that the pictures bottom and top left on page 18 are taken in the garden there. The delightful picture (above) shows the family playing croquet with the paraphernalia of day-to-day life evident. An ornamental urn and statuary in the background complement the onions drying in the sun.

These family photographs were taken about 1870. From the 1871 census we learn that Myrtle House was pretty crowded, perhaps because in the 1860s Date had taken to letting apartments. He was absent on the night of the census but in the house were his wife, Elizabeth, Mary and Annie, by then married to a master mariner who was doubtless at sea, and her six-month-old son, William James. Two other grandchildren were staying, Clara (11) and Sydney Stoate (9), children of one of the sons who had become a commercial traveller. The Dates employed a general servant, Selina Jones, and lodgers and visitors included Henry Smallwood (26), Wesleyan minister, and Jane Taylor (20), a farmer's daughter.

In the pictures opposite it is likely that Mary and Annie are seen with their parents and below a grandchild poses with one of the sons.

The photograph below is labelled Alcombe and could be the rear of Alcombe Cottage, now Hoar Oak House. No personal Date link has yet been established with this photograph but the serenity of the picture with baskets in the foreground ready for picking apples from the dwarf trees makes it an exceptional example of Date's work.

LYDEARD ST LAWRENCE

This fascinating photograph appears to show work in progress on decorating a reception area in front of an end-on marquee. A man, centre top, seems to be helping with the decorating under the supervision of a number of young ladies in elegant crinolines. We have not been able to identify the people in the photograph but they may be members of one of several clergy families living in the village at the time. The set pieces in the foreground include a cow which may indicate that this was a meeting of a local Agricultural Association founded c.1860 to encourage farm labourers and their families to work hard, save hard, and live abstemious lives. In the first few years it was a great success!

THE PARISH OF
WEST QUANTOXHEAD
St Audries

St Audries House before its renovation in c.1870 (below, right). In the picture above can be seen the new front. The conservatory on the right was moved forward when the house was altered. Heaps of stone on the left indicate that the building work had only recently been completed.

This charming picture of the Orangery with gardeners and gentry admiring the hothouse plants was taken in c.1870. The parapet has since been lowered. In the smaller picture we can see into the Orangery from an adjoining entrance hall.

Looking towards the church from the old rectory drive.

St Audries School built by Sir Alexander Acland Hood in 1857.

Two charming ladies, one holding her parasol, pose to be photographed by James Date at West Quantoxhead. The Parish Church of St Etheldreda can be seen in the background. Might the ladies have been members of the Acland Hood family who lived at St Audries House nearby? It was this family who financed the building of this graceful church in 1856.

The church of St Etheldreda was rebuilt to a design by London architect, John Norton (the architect of Tyntesfield in North Somerset recently acquired by the National Trust). There must have been problems, perhaps financial, because the building does not incorporate everything shown in the original plans. It was consecrated on 17 October 1856. In the background on the left of the lower picture can be seen the gravestones cleared from the churchyard when the new church was built.

Home Farm, built in 1855. To the left are Seaview Cottages and to the right can be seen a driveway sweeping round to the mansion house and church.

The Goyle in the woods near Home Farm. This was part of the landscaping of the grounds that took place in c.1860. Remains of the steps and pillars can still be seen.

The waterfall below Home Farm is known as St Etheldreda's Fall.

Weacombe

Weacombe House in the 1860s. The house was built some time between 1750 and 1770 for J.C. Luxton. It was later bought by Mrs St Albyn of Alfoxden and by the 1860s was occupied by Langley St Albyn. For a few years it was occupied by various tenants until it was bought in c.1871 by the Revd Ottiwell Sadler who had been the rector of Brancaster. The small central block with balcony was a later addition but the buildings to the rear were the original domestic offices. Both the balcony and the glasshouses to the right eventually fell down! In the background is Weacombe Farm.

As yet we have not identified this man but wonder whether he is Langley St Albyn.

A well-groomed horse waits patiently with the brougham outside Weacombe House.

Weacombe Farm in the 1860s. This house, built in the early-eighteenth century, may have originally been the site of the main house of the manor. At the time the photograph was taken Miss Mary Moore was the farmer. She was succeeded by 1872 by William Roberts. The farm was a popular venue for Methodist Sunday School outings in the 1870s. Later the farm was occupied by members of the Kingsbury family.

The cottages in the combe at Weacombe shown in this and the following photograph were all demolished some while ago. They all appear on an estate map of c.1800. A small portion of wall built into a modern garage and stray garden flowers are all that remain of the cottage on the right known as Palmers. To the left is the group of cottages shown below and in the distance is a small cottage known as Poors Cottage.

It is thought that these cottages were demolished in the late-nineteenth century to make room for a house for the head gardener at Weacombe. Two estate cottages were built nearby in the twentieth century.

THE PARISH OF ST DECUMAN

Doniford

Swillbridge House, c.1870. In the eighteenth and nineteenth centuries the Pulman family made blankets at Doniford on the site of an earlier fulling-mill and the mill was still in production in 1841. The mill buildings stood beside a leat fed by the Doniford stream, with adjoining fields known as Rack Meadow where the cloth was stretched to dry, included the miller's house of which Swillbridge House was a part. For a while in the first half of the twentieth century Major-General L.C. Dunsterville, model for Rudyard Kipling's 'Stalky', lived at Swillbridge.

Watchet

Watchet Harbour – Trucks of iron ore from the Brendon Hill mines are ready for loading into the little sailing ships waiting alongside the iron-ore jetty, 1860s. The jetty was situated on the western side of the harbour.

Looking seaward from a field with stooks of corn across Brendon Road. In the foreground are Thorne's Sawmills. Timber brought by horse-drawn wagons is piled ready to be sawn into planks. In the centre left is the first Methodist chapel and behind is the chimney of Gliddon's foundry. The thatched house (centre) is the residence of James Date.

A small group of children sit on the newly constructed East Pier, 1862. The Western Pier on the left was at that time of wooden construction. The hexagonal iron tower of the lighthouse cost £75. During a horrendous storm in December 1900 the wooden pier was completely destroyed and was rebuilt later in masonry. Fortunately the little lighthouse survived the storm and today it guides visiting yachts into the marina.

A photograph of the busy harbour taken from the footpath leading to the Pleasure Ground on the headland above, 1860s.

This 1860s view of the harbour shows some ships with their canvas sails hoisted, although the tide is out. The reason for this was to dry the sails to avoid damage by mildew. In the foreground a gentleman is standing at the top of a slipway leading to the beach. The slipway was later destroyed by storms and an alternate access to the beach was provided by means of stone steps which exist to this day.

The western end of the Esplanade, 1860s, with a row of posts to prevent access by vehicular traffic. Later a gate was erected to allow for the transportation of the lifeboat on its carriage to the harbour slipway. The old Market House with its bell turret shown on the right now houses the Town Museum, with Holy Cross Chapel above.

Horse-drawn wagons have brought sacks of flour from Stoate's Flour Mills to be loaded into the ships waiting below, 1860s.

Close-up view of Watchet Paper Mill. The 1871 census records that at that time the mill employed 26 men, 23 women and 10 boys. The prominent residence on the hill above was the home of the mill's proprietor, Alfred Wansborough, and was known as Belmont Villa.

Watchet Lifeboat House was built in 1874 on a plot of land donated by the Countess of Egremont. It cost £352 to build. The first rowing and sailing lifeboat was financed by Mrs Soames of Torrington and was named Joseph Soames *after her late husband. In 1944 the station was closed. The building was altered and its elegant upper façade removed when it was converted into the Town Library in 1953. The cost of this was born by Mr Leonard L. Stoate of Bristol.*

The newly built Church of England School with headmaster's house on the left, 1874. (It is now in use as the Baptist Church.) In 1909 another school was built by the County Council in the field in the foreground. Both schools were closed after a larger modern school was built at Liddymore Road in 1990. Later the Council School was demolished and the site developed as a housing estate known today as School Close.

This photograph was taken near the top of the slipway leading to the beach at West Street, c.1880. A limekiln and a number of old cottages were demolished at that time. In 1887 a new row of houses was erected on the site and given the name of Jubilee Terrace. This was to commemorate the Golden Jubilee of Queen Victoria. The 1887 date stone can still be seen built into the wall of No. 71 West Street.

This house at the top end of Swain Street was for many years the home of photographer James Date. With its thatched roof and beautiful floral display, including myrtle shrubs, it was known as Myrtle House. The building on the far left, also thatched, is the Anchor Inn in Anchor Street.

Looking down Swain Street, 1860s. The practising chemist at that time was William Harris. The same premises have continued in use as a pharmacy to the present day.

The building shown in the centre of the photograph was originally the old Wesleyan Church located off Swain Street. The premises were subsequently taken over by the Salvation Army and the first officers to be appointed on 31 July 1884 were a Captain Castle and Lieutenant Hall. Since then the building has been affectionately called Castle Hall and is, at the time of writing, the headquarters of the 1st Watchet Sea Scouts Group.

This photograph was taken on the occasion of the official opening of Watchet railway station when the first passenger train arrived from Taunton on 31 March 1862. The triumphal arch decorating the station building declares: 'Welcome ye friends of progress'. It was reported that it was a day of great celebration in the town with brass bands and a sumptuous dinner in the evening.

This splendid photograph of the Wesleyan Methodist Chapel is taken from the railway station platform. Note in the foreground the broad-gauge railway lines with trucks loaded for despatch and also the weighbridge building, 1870s.

This lane beside St Decumans Church gives pedestrian access to St Decumans Holy Well. According to a quaint old legend the water from this well possessed miraculous healing powers, made good use of by St Decuman himself, even after he was beheaded by local infidels in the seventh century. After years of neglect, the well has recently been restored and made accessible thanks mainly to the efforts of the present vicar, the Reverend David Ireson. A way-marked footpath leads from the end of the lane to the historic house of Kentsford and then onward to join the old Mineral Line footpath to Washford or Watchet.

High on a hill overlooking Watchet is the handsome Parish Church of St Decumans, parts of which date from the thirteenth century. In R.D. Blackmore's romantic novel **Lorna Doone,** *the mother of the heroine is said to have been buried in Watchet churchyard. Furthermore, the renowned poet, Samuel Taylor Coleridge, in 'The Rime of the Ancient Mariner' refers to Watchet's church on the hill above the harbour from where his ancient mariner set sail.*

A penny for the thoughts of the two likely lads sitting on the steps of the fifteenth-century churchyard cross in St Decumans churchyard, 1880s.

One might wonder why James Date photographed this railed-off plot in St Decumans churchyard. It contained the graves of members of the Stoate family who died during the nineteenth century. The answer can be found on one of the several tombstones which reads: Elizabeth Date died in 1874 at the age of 62 years. She was a member of the Stoate family and was the wife of the photographer. James Date's name was also added to the tombstone after he died in 1895 aged 89 years.

The interior of St Decumans Church with elaborate floral decorations. The text above the screen indicates the celebration of Christmas. The old-fashioned box pews shown were removed in 1884 when church renovations were carried out by the well-known architect, J. Piers St Aubyn. The pulpit shown here on the right was moved to a new position on the left in 1896.

The side chapel on the north side of the choir stalls contains tombs and monuments to the eminent Wyndham family. A gruesome old legend suggests that in 1559 Lady Florence Wyndham, mistakenly believed to be dead, was laid to rest in one of the family tombs. Fortunately she was awakened from her trance by a grave robber who endeavoured to remove her golden wedding ring. Attired only in her burial shroud, Lady Wyndham returned to her home and husband at Kentsford. Some time later she gave birth to a son named John and from him the Wyndham line continues to this day.

The Wesleyan Methodist Chapel situated in Harbour Road, Watchet was built in 1871 by contractors John Pearce of Minehead for the sum of £2,100. Geometrical in style, it was sufficiently large to accommodate 500 worshippers whilst underneath the chapel there was a large schoolroom with ancillary rooms for 400 persons, together with a chapel-keeper's house at the back. Centrally situated, the chapel continues its witness and the schoolroom is extensively used by other organisations in the town.

Mr Jack Binding, a lifelong Methodist, thinks that this photograph, of a group outside the Wesleyan Chapel, was possibly taken on the occasion of an annual meeting of Synod when clergy and lay members from surrounding circuits would gather together to formulate the ongoing work of the Church.

From 1862 until 1874 when the railway was extended to Minehead, Watchet was the terminus for the Bristol and Exeter Railway's branch line from Taunton. The layout of the broad-gauge tracks is clearly shown. Note the engine shed, water tower and the disc and crossbar signal. Newly built Causeway Terrace (1859) can be seen top left. Coastguards lived in four of the cottages at the top end.

This photograph was taken shortly after the Methodist Chapel was built in 1871. The large house abutting on to the Esplanade and the buildings to the left of it all formed part of a farm which was known at one time as Beach Farm, c.1872.

A wooden footbridge crosses the railway line near the station, 1870s. The goods shed, now the Watchet Boat Museum, is situated just behind.

Because of its proximity to the Parish Church, Watchet's Paper Mill was known for many years as St Decumans Paper Mill. The route of the West Somerset Mineral Railway ran parallel with the wooden fence in the foreground.

A gentleman enjoys the view of the town from the headlands above the harbour. The Egremont Trustees gave a fair-sized area of land here to the townsfolk in the 1860s. It was known as the Pleasure Ground and seats were provided by public subscription. A thatched refreshment room was also erected but some years later it was burnt down.

View of the old town from fields above New Road, now known as Brendon Road. The square section off the road was known as 'cracking stones'. It was here that stones were manually and laboriously cracked with a hammer for road making. Water flowing through the mill leet on the left provided power by means of a water-wheel to grind corn at Stoate's main Flour Mill. The tall building top centre is Melbourne House in Market Street, 1870s.

Cows from Mill Farm graze in 'the Croft' beside Stoate's Flour Mill off Anchor Street. The chimney-stack indicates that by this time (1885) the mill had been updated and needed coal-fired steam power to augment its water-wheel power. Sad to relate this mill was destroyed by fire in 1911 and the whole business moved to Bristol.

From a position high on Cleeve Hill, James Date captured this delightful view between the trees of the Paper Mill overlooked by the Parish Church, c.1870.

These six sailing vessels have discharged their cargoes of coal manually into horse-drawn carts, one of which is just discernible alongside the second ship from the left. When the tide returned, the ships would in turn have been moved alongside the iron-ore jetty behind them. Truckloads of ore would then be tipped into each vessel's hold by means of the loading chutes that can be seen in the raised position. The little vessel third from the left is the smack Tom *owned by John Thorne, 1870s.*

In the early 1860s much timber was imported and some was used for the constructions of the western breakwater. The large brig in the foreground has unloaded a part of her cargo of sawn timber into a horse-drawn wagon. This would have been brought ashore by way of the slipway on the right. Smoke or steam issuing from the chimney-stack on the left is from Thorne's Steam Sawmills situated near The Cross. The row of cottages on the right were known as The Folly and renamed later as Channel View.

THE PARISH OF ST DECUMAN

Watchet Esplanade almost deserted except for an invalid seated in her Bath chair and attended by her maid, 1870s. Note the absence of safety railings along the edge. One dark night a couple of drunken sailors fell over the edge into the harbour. Fortunately they could both swim and came to no harm. In 1907 safety railings, financed by a public-spirited organisation known as the Watchet Sports Committee, were erected.

The engine driver, fireman and guard, as well as the staff of the Watchet station, stand proudly on or beside the broad-gauge locomotive No. 68 which has arrived from Taunton, c.1867

Watchet, as well as being the terminus of the Bristol and Exeter branch line from Taunton, was also the end station of the quite separate West Somerset Mineral Railway which brought iron ore and passengers from the Brendon Hills. The thatched cottage (centre) is situated in Mill Lane and is known today as Lyn Cottage. The buildings to the left of it are the old Manor Corn Mill, operated by the Stoate family, and the Star Inn.

'There's nothing quite like it for cooling the blood', they say. But the residents of Swain Street, as this picture shows, had more than their fair share of glorious mud in the 1860s. Some of it could be avoided by making use of the crude stepping-stones on the pavement. The boot-scrapers (bottom left) would certainly have been well used. Note the top-hatted policeman standing outside the chemist's shop, the tall building on the right.

This picturesque little stone bridge spanned the river approximately 100 yards upstream of the present road bridge leading to Whitehall. It gave access to the thatched Mill Farmhouse, the home of the Nicholas family, shown on the right. The house was destroyed by fire in 1951. Ten years later, as a precautionary measure to prevent flooding, the little stone bridge was demolished and replaced by the less attractive single-span structure of today.

Part of old Watchet town viewed from a field above Brendon Road. The nearest buildings on the left form part of Mill Farm, which ceased to operate as such from the early 1970s. The thatched cottages to the right of them are on the south side of Anchor Street and include the Anchor Inn. Two large chimney-stacks can be seen on the right; the furthest away served Gliddon's Iron Foundry. The other on the near right belonged to Thorne's Steam Sawmills, c.1860s.

Looking down Swain Street, 1860s. The buildings on the right were used for agricultural purposes and as a coal depot. In the early 1930s the site was cleared and redeveloped with a garage and shops on the ground floor and a cinema, known as the Cosy Cinema, as well as a ballroom on the floor above. Later it was a Van Heusen shirt factory. The building today is used by a group of doctors as a health centre for the town.

A small gathering of unknown people pose for their photograph at the top of Swain Street, 1860s. We shall probably never know the identity of the top-hatted gentlemen nor that of the dignitary seated in the pony-drawn trap and, even less likely, that of the two little urchins on the right. Might they have been instructed by James Date to keep perfectly still and to watch for the dickybird? The thatched property behind the group is now the Town Council Offices.

These fife and drum bandsmen and boys pose for their photograph on the rocky beach at Watchet. Quite a number of people can be seen on the beach behind them. Two daring lads have clambered on to a rocky ledge of the alabaster cliffs. Watchet has always been a town of music and several bands have existed from the mid-nineteenth century. Even today, Watchet can boast two prize-winning brass bands, a choral society and a uniformed Town Crier who, like his famous predecessor, shantyman Yankee Jack, has a powerful and melodious voice.

Another photograph of the youthful fife and drum band performing in an unidentified but seemingly well-watered flower garden.

To capture this most delightful photo-graph, James Date set up his camera looking downstream on the old pack-horse bridge next to the thatched cottages in Mill Street. The top-hatted gentleman and small lad are fishing in the river, probably for eels. The sluice gates in the foreground have been lowered, thus raising and directing the river water into the mill leet behind them. By means of a water-wheel, it provided power to grind corn in Stoate's old Manor Mill further downstream, c.1860s

5

❧ WILLITON ❧

View over Williton, c.1870

Williton Methodist Chapel, the minister's house and schoolroom on Tower Hill replaced an earlier chapel in Fore Street. Work by builders J. Chibbet & Sons began in 1883 and cost £4,500. The chapel was opened in May 1884

Orchard Wyndham, c.1880, the seat of the Wyndham family since 1529. The heart of the house is the original medieval hall, which is surrounded by additions made from the fifteenth to the nineteenth centuries.

Orchard Wyndham estate lodge, now the estate office. It looks as if the builders were just completing work on the house and James Date may have been called over to record the event.

Williton Police Station was built before 1872 and included accommodation for the superintendent and sergeant, cells and a courtroom.

St Peter's Church, rebuilt and enlarged in 1857/8. The spire is thought to have been lost in a gale, c.1870, which helps to date the picture. Until 1902 Williton was part of the parish of St Decuman and there was only a chapel-of-ease at Williton. The first chapel on the site was that founded by Robert Fitzurse, brother of Sir Reginald who was lord of the manor of Williton and one of the four murderers of Thomas à Becket in 1170.

MONKSILVER & NETTLECOMBE
Monksilver

This memorial in Monksilver churchyard was erected by the parishioners in the mid-1860s to the memory of William Francis Chilcott, curate for 15 years and rector for 20 years, and his wife, Frances. It is often known as the Village Cross. It is probable that these photographs were taken to record the erection of the cross.

The old rectory at Monksilver, now a private house. This thatched house, with a touch of Strawberry Hill Gothic, was planned in 1838 though by 1910 it was 'derelict'. This photograph may have been taken when the forthright William Meade King was rector. He occupied the living for some 27 years and died in 1896. We have not been able to identify the children.

Nettlecombe

Nettlecombe Court, the home of the Trevelyan family from the late 1400s, and St Mary's Church, c.1875. The house was reconstructed c.1600 by John Trevelyan. The most unusual thing about this picture is that it shows the house plastered and limewashed whereas today it is red sandstone. Once Nettlecombe village stood on the green but during the later 1700s it was gradually moved to make way for improvements to the house and landscaping of the grounds.

This piece of water, first thought to be the ornamental pond at Nettlecombe, seems more likely to be one of the ponds at Huish Barton which were turned into ornamental lakes at some unidentified date. There is still a tree on a small island in the centre of the largest pond there.

Looking down to the Court and church through grounds landscaped by John Veitch in 1792.

*A gate leading to the walk up to Parsonage
Pond.*

Combe Cottage set in the countryside below Combe House.

Combe House was Nettlecombe's rectory until 1922. It was built as a new parsonage house soon after 1797 on the Lawn in Pooke Wood. This photograph may have been taken when Hugh Willoughby Jermyn, rector of the parish from 1858–70, held the living.

❧ THE PARISH OF ❧ OLD CLEEVE

Comberow and Brendon Hill

With engine driver Nicholas Redd at the controls, the locomotive, 'Pontypool', is about to leave Watchet's Mineral Railway Station en route to Washford, Roadwater and Comberow. The horse was used to haul trucks of iron ore from the station to the loading chutes on the jetty, c.1875. Although this photograph was taken in Watchet, it sets the scene for the views that follow.

Views of Comberow station at the foot of the incline on the West Somerset Mineral Railway. The line was built in the 1850s to carry iron ore from the Brendon Hill mines to Watchet harbour. The line to Comberow was completed by December 1857, but although the incline was opened on 31 May 1858 it was not completed with its winding gear installed until March 1861. The line to Comberow was opened to passengers in 1865 but if they wished to travel up the incline they did so at their own risk

This well-known picture taken on the incline shows Comberow from above, c.1875. The man in the centre may well have been walking up the incline when persuaded by the photographer to pose on the line thus adding proportion and interest to the picture.

This photograph shows the full extent of the incline, three-quarters of a mile long and with a gradient of 1:4. The house on the left was the stationmaster's house with Comberow Farm on the right.

Langham Hill Mine, c.1870, showing the aerial ropeway from Kennesome Mine.

The waterfall, close to the incline, which may have incorporated a drainage system from the Carnarvon mine.

Naked Boy Stone stands on the Brendon Hills at a point near where four parishes meet – Brompton Regis, Clatworthy, Huish Champflower and Old Cleeve. Many people consider it to be a boundary stone and assume that its name refers to the practice of beating the bounds when, on an annual perambulation of the parish boundaries, boys were 'beaten' to ensure they remembered where those boundaries were. However, Dr Robert Dunning, editor of the Victoria County History, *notes that the accurate county map of Christopher Greenwood of 1822 marks the spot as 'Fournaked boys'. He tells us that down in the valley towards the coast half way between Old Cleeve village and Withycombe, but still in Old Cleeve parish, was a little farm called Fernacre. The name was recorded before the end of the twelfth century and the farm was part of the foundation estate of Cleeve Abbey. It was scattered across the parish, with meadow at Fernacre itself, arable at Croydon above Roadwater, and rough pasture at Stamborough on the way to Leigh Barton. He goes on: 'It seems entirely reasonable that there was also woodland to provide fuel for the estate where there is still woodland on the steepest slopes reaching up to Sminhays and the incline. This, surely, is Fernacre wood, Fernacre bois, Fournaked boys.'*

Washford

The Wesleyan chapel and schoolroom at Washford. The chapel was built in 1824 at a cost of £400 and over the next 25 years there were various additions, making it the largest chapel in the Circuit for a time. A day school was opened in 1869 and in 1872 G.H. Bryant was the Master and Mrs Julia Bryant the Mistress. Other Masters included Samuel Noall, George Taylor and R. Blackburn. The school closed c.1880 for lack of support.

Cleeve Abbey

This Cistercian abbey was founded in c.1198 and by the sixteenth century included granges at nearby Binham, Stout (Hungerford), Croydon, Linton and Leigh Barton. In spite of pleas for the abbey to be saved, it was dissolved in 1536 and the lands passed to the Earl of Sussex while the abbey buildings themselves were rented by Anthony Busterd. The church was pulled down and some of the stone used in new buildings in the neighbourhood. The remaining buildings were turned over to farm use. By 1794, when the abbey and estates were put up for sale, the former abbey buildings included a brewhouse, granary, pig cots, a large barn over them, a good barn on the ground floor and many storerooms. An arched gateway (the gatehouse) served as a cart-house.

When in 1875 Mr G.F. Luttrell of Dunster Castle bought the abbey ruins the site was one of 'complete desecration and foulness'. The ground plan of the abbey with which we are so familiar today was completely hidden beneath 'huge ancient fragments of rubble, toppled over... a considerable depth of heavy soil and beach-stone... to say nothing of an Augean mass of farm ordure at the east end.' The photographs that follow were taken at about this time.

The chapter house. Note the wall beyond the arch dividing the cloister and the supports for harvest wagons stored against the walls.

The gatehouse with farm buildings, now demolished, and the leat to the fish-pond.

Looking north across the cloister garth to the covered cloister passage.

Looking across the cloister garth to the sixteenth-century refectory.

The gated entrance to the chapter house seen from the cloisters and, on the right, the stair to the dorter.

The abbey gatehouse in use as a cart-house

The ivy-hung sixteenth-century refectory. In the foreground the medieval tiled floor of an earlier refectory is smothered with vegetation. In c.1885 it was excavated by archaeologists and when men removed the earth they found, more than two feet below the surface, a 'splendid specimen of a tessellated pavement', 40 feet long, 14 feet broad, covered with heraldic tiles of seven or eight designs. At first a glazed frame was placed over the tiles to protect them, but the heat of the sun cracked and damaged the tiles so the frame was replaced by a layer of sawdust which could easily be brushed aside so that visitors could view the floor.

Old Cleeve

The Church Room on the right was used as a poorhouse in the eighteenth century and then in 1811 the rector opened a school in the premises which continued until 1855. Once upon a time villagers who could not read gathered here to listen to Mr Bill Mogg reading from the West Somerset Free Press. The lychgate, so familiar today, was erected by Messrs W. Harrison in 1892.

The Norman church of St Andrew's, Old Cleeve was altered in the fifteenth century and eventually restored. The tower was part-funded by wool merchant John Tucker of Dunster and parishioners in 1533.

Myrtle Cottage, built in 1468, the oldest cottage in Old Cleeve.

The old rectory built in 1728 by James Newton who became rector of the parish that year and built the house on an earlier site. It was sold in 1937 and is now a retirement home. The drive swept down to the stables, now Mellory, and emerged somewhere opposite the present rectory.

Looking towards the west door of the church.

COASTAL VIEWS FROM WATCHET TO BLUE ANCHOR

In his handbook to Watchet published in 1867, James Date enthused about the coast between Watchet and Blue Anchor:

The coast scenery is of singular beauty. The alabaster rocks are very magnificent and attractive, especially when seen with a favourable light – the variegated sparkling strata are very fine. These rocks rise with prodigious magnificence, and are much admired for their bold and commanding position, being almost perpendicular from the sea, whose maddened waves have torn their fronts into misshaped crags, and scooped their sides into stupendous caverns. The detached masses, by their picturesque forms, add to the interest of the scene. Further west are the Blue Anchor rocks, composed principally of the grey alabaster, used for manure. This rock scenery, with the fossil remains found embedded in the Blue Lias ridges of this shore, must surely recommend the area to visitors.

It is clear from Date's photographs that people enjoyed walks and picnics on the seashore.

Ice on the cliffs during a particularly cold winter.

This stack at the Blue Anchor end of the beach collapsed at least a century ago.

BLUE ANCHOR
& CARHAMPTON
Blue Anchor

Blue Anchor, c.1865. At this time the area was known as Cleeve Bay. In the background is the Blue Anchor Inn while in the foreground are the brickworks that were managed by Robert Henson, innkeeper at the inn during the 1860s. To the right can be seen the brick kiln with wings used for storage. To their left are stacks of bricks. Bricks were hand-moulded and the clay was obtained from nearby claypits. The road seen on the left was the toll-road that ran along the top of the beach to Watchet and Bridgwater. The houses between – note the farm with hayrick in the yard – were demolished by the end of the century. It is hard to identify the toll-house but it may be in the centre of this group of houses or alternatively out of view. On the left are small fishing boats pulled up on to the beach.

View over the farm to North Hill, Minehead, c.1865.

View across Cleeve Bay to Dunster and Minehead. From this photograph it is clear that the farm and cottages were right on the beach. The wooden groynes were an early form of sea defence but there was no sea wall so the toll-road must have been liable to flooding.

Carhampton

St John the Baptist Church, Carhampton, c.1865. Although the body of the church has been restored, the simple tower topped with a wooden structure and shingle roof has yet to be rebuilt. Until c.1830 the 'main' road ran through the churchyard and the trackway can be seen in the foreground.

St John the Baptist Church, Carhampton, c.1871. The church tower was rebuilt of red sandstone in 1870. The clockface does not seem to have been replaced yet which may indicate that the work has only just been completed. The remains of a medieval preaching cross can be seen in the centre of the picture.

⚮ THE PARISH OF ⚮ DUNSTER

View from Grabbist Hill to Conygar Hill and Conygar Tower in the distance. The tower and its accompanying ruined 'Roman' arches were built by Henry Fownes Luttrell in 1775 as a folly set in a pleasure ground. Although by the 1870s trees covered the hill, it was still a popular place for walkers.

This panoramic view of the castle taken some time before the castle was remodelled (1868–72) shows, from the left, Dunster Mill, the Rustic Bridge, in front The Lawns and, to the right, the Palladian (or Lawns) Bridge.

View of Conygar Hill showing Conygar Tower and in the foreground the pottery kiln in the grounds of the Luttrell Arms Hotel. The kiln was being used in the mid-1700s and is thought to be the oldest extant kiln in the country.

The Yarn Market and High Street at Dunster before 1872. On the left is the Luttrell Arms Hotel, Family and Commercial Hotel and Posting House. John Withycombe was the proprietor. On the right is a general shop and warehouse and beyond the Horse and Crook Inn.

This photograph of part of Dunster High Street taken c.1865 shows the varied roof lines and building styles that still contribute to Dunster's charm today. In the centre of the picture is the George Inn, kept by Charles Lang. Mr John Bennet was a hatter while Robert Hole, next door, was a builder and cabinet maker who also kept an ironmongery if the tools standing outside are anything to go by.

Priory Farm, Dunster. A straw rick takes pride of place in the farmyard behind the church some time before 1868 when the old vicarage, known as the Priory, was built nearby. In the middle ground are the farm buildings of the Home Farm.

This view across the village to the castle was taken before the castle was remodelled, 1868–72. It is photographed from the foot of Conygar Hill with the present Priory Gate House and Hole's cottages in the foreground. Towards the back on the right can be seen the Castle's early-seventeenth-century stables.

St George's Church has been photographed across a roofscape of houses and farm buildings in Church Street, West Street and at the foot of Castle Hill. It is worthy of any Tuscan scene today! In the centre is the general dealers which, in the later Victorian period, was run by Amors and which in 1901 was taken over by J.H. Parham. Behind the church can be seen the vicarage, newly built and with some scaffolding still in place. This helps us to date the photograph to some time soon after 1868 when Piers St Aubyn designed the house.

A view over Home Farm and the Tithe Barn complex of buildings from the foot of Conygar Hill some time after the castle was restored in 1872.

Priory Farm, Dunster. These farm buildings, many demolished about 1868 when the new vicarage was built, were part of the farm established on the grounds of the medieval Benedictine priory after it was dissolved in 1537. The timber and the position of the men suggests that they are working in a sawpit.

We have not been able to identify the exact site of this bridge and sluice gate on the River Avill at Dunster.

The new vicarage at Dunster, designed by Piers St Aubyn, photographed during the completion of the work some time between 1868 and 1870. The house, often known as the Old Priory, was built on land formerly occupied by Priory Farm. The workmen pose proudly in front of the house, tools and dress indicating some of their occupations.

The Palladian or Lawns Bridge. The wooden fence and gates, no longer in existence, complement the angles of the bridge.

These bridges were built as part of the land-scaping of the castle grounds and park by Henry Fownes Luttrell in the mid-1700s

The Rustic Bridge.

Dunster Castle Gatehouse was built by Sir Hugh Luttrell, the first of the family to live in the castle, in 1420. Photographed from the steep approach road, there is a particular beauty about the oval shape created by the arch and reflected by the wooden gates. The person approaching the Gatehouse in the photograph below may well be an artist with his bag of paints and brushes on his back.

Dunster Gatehouse photographed from the Green in front of the castle.

Dunster Castle before its remodelling. In 1868, George Fownes Luttrell employed the architect Anthony Salvin to draw up designs for the restoration of the castle. The building seen here is that redesigned in Jacobean style by William Arnold, the architect of Montacute House, soon after 1617.

Dunster Castle soon after its remodelling in 1868–72. The architect, Anthony Salvin, aimed to make the castle appear to be a medieval building that had been altered over the centuries. The heap of stones to the left may indicate that the work was not yet complete.

West Street, Dunster, c.1875. James Date had a yet-to-be-identified studio in West Street (see Introduction page 13) and the authors wonder whether it was sited behind this shop. On the left facing up the street is the house used as the parish workhouse in the eighteenth and early-nineteenth centuries.

In 1858, a 'new and very handsome' police station and magistrates' court was built on an open site at the foot of Dunster Steep to a design by Piers St Aubyn. Petty Sessions were held here every Friday but particularly on the first Friday of the month. The station included living accommodation for a superintendent and sergeant and its gardens were extensive. Today houses cram up against the building while the road has been widened to pass the building more closely.

❧ THE PARISH OF ❧ MINEHEAD

Higher Town, Minehead, c.1875. This view is taken from above Postboy with Lower Moor Farm on the left. Thatched cottages in Church Town and allotments spread to the right.

The first buildings in the Parks viewed from Ball Park, c.1875. The block of houses to the left were built before 1861 and include Mentone which, in the 1890s, was rented in the summer by Mr Forman, a master at Repton College, whose daughter Rosamond was later to marry Geoffrey Fisher who became Archbishop of Canterbury. To the right is the Baptist chapel built in the 1830s. The fields behind on North Hill are hedged and used as pasture.

Church Steps with St Michael's Church in the background, c.1880. In the middle foreground are the premises of Slades, Monumental Masons, while just behind them is the old workhouse which housed the poor of the town until a new workhouse was built in Middle Street in 1821. To the right is the house of Clerk Lewry who kept a school in a room at the back of the house. Although crippled he kept good discipline with the help of a flying ruler!

A similar view to that on page 93 taken from a different angle

Looking up the Parade to the Plume of Feathers, pre-1870. On the right is the old Fish Market with myrtle-clad houses built after 1791 to replace the houses that were burnt during the fire of that year. The trees indicate a new civic pride. In 1861 market day was Wednesday when the Market House was open for the sale of meat and provisions. On the left is Stuckey's Bank designed by Piers St Aubyn, c.1869.

Probably taken on the same visit, James Date has carefully grouped figures to add focus to the picture. In the background is the Plume of Feathers with its original main entrance facing down the Parade. Mrs Ann Greensill kept the Feathers at about this time.

This photograph, found in James Date's contact album, is later than most of his photographs and may not have been his work. It provides an interesting contrast to the previous photographs. The buildings on the right, designed by Piers St Aubyn, were built c.1882.

Minehead station in broad-gauge days with the engine shed on the right. The railway reached Minehead in 1874 and the track was converted to standard gauge in October 1882.

Another view of Minehead station showing the station and platform with the newly built Esplanade behind.

The station when first built had little protection from the sea. This photograph looks from the beach to the Esplanade, in the closing stages of building, with, on the left, the railway. In the foreground is a beach hut on wheels.

Nos 1–4 the Esplanade was the first new building on the sea front. It was designed by Piers St Aubyn for Thomas Ponsford and was built in 1875. This photograph is taken from across the present Avenue before there were any other buildings.

The Beach Hotel, built by Mr George Fownes Luttrell in 1875 to designs by either Piers St Aubyn or C.H. Samson, the Luttrell's Building Bailiff, and the Esplanade from the beach. Sand dunes can today only be found near the golf course.

Looking across to North Hill, c.1875. There are no new buildings on North Hill where the field pattern reflects that of medieval times. Note the simple but effective sea defences in the foreground.

These beautifully composed photographs show North Hill and the beach at Minehead before any new building, c.1875. The lower fields formed part of the medieval North Field and the markings in the lower fields show there was once medieval strip-farming. The path along the top of the beach was a concession to visitors. The houses on the left which probably included Ridler's timber and coal yard were demolished later in the century to make way for new building.

This photograph shows the rear of Lamb Cottage near the junction of New (Blenheim) Road and Quay Street, c.1875. The important timber business of the Ridler family, centred at their timber yard nearby, existed prior to 1843, and was concerned with the export of locally-grown hardwoods and the import of softwoods from Canada. The timber on the beach may be waiting to be shipped.

This view from North Hill, c.1875, shows Quay Street to the left foreground and, in the background, the railway, the Beach Hotel and the Esplanade. It is clear from this photograph that Minehead's economy was still based on agriculture.

A close-up showing part of Quay Street with houses and gardens on either side of the road. In the centre facing down the street is Lamb Cottage. Beyond the fields can be seen the Esplanade, the Beach Hotel and, far left, the station.

Part of Quay Street, Minehead, c.1875.

A house almost certainly in Quay Street, c.1875. The horse pulls a cart loaded with seaweed to be used as fertiliser on the land.

A cottage near the sea beyond the harbour with North Hill rising behind.

Minehead Harbour, c.1875. Timber shown in the foreground was shipped to South Wales to make pit props. In the background can be seen the Bristol Channel Chemical Works established by Thomas Lomas in c.1875. He tried unsuccessfully to build a house above the works but was compelled to move to a new site and two years later Cleveland, a two-storey house above the church on North Hill, built in brick and timber in Jacobean style, was completed for the Lomas family. These boats are, according to John Gilman in Exmoor's Maritime Heritage, *'rural smacks' wind-bound in the harbour, and behind is the Customs House. The big warehouse, today Tides Reach flats, has not yet been built.*

WEST OF PORLOCK

Porlock Weir

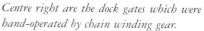

Porlock Weir. The dock at the weir with small boats pulled up on the shingle.

Centre right are the dock gates which were hand-operated by chain winding gear.

Porlock Weir, c.1875, showing the Anchor Hotel with a thatched building to the left that was demolished in 1902 to make way for a two-gable extension. To the middle left is the Ship Inn. To the left is the building that was to become the Cottage Hotel.

Culbone

The tiny Culbone church, c.1860, with visitors behaving badly! It is likely that James Date invited his friend to sit on the stump of the cross to make a more interesting picture.

There is nowhere today at Culbone where these views up the valley could be photographed. The cleared land near the church, used perhaps for pasture, gardens or allotments, may indicate that there were other cleared fields from which these photographs could have been taken.

Lynmouth

Lynmouth showing Mars Hill and the Rhenish Tower before the late 1880s and probably in the 1860s or 1870s.

The Valley of the Rocks, popular with visitors from the 1790s. We often assume that the rocks never change but the profile shown here cannot be seen today.

Ilfracombe

Cheyne Beach in c.1870 with Lantern Hill and Hillsborough behind to the right.

Cheyne Beach. The spire of St Philip and St James Church, built in 1856, can be seen to the left with Capstone Hill to the right. The houses above are on Compass Hill.

❧ FURTHER AFIELD ❧

James Date seems to have visited a number of popular tourist destinations, perhaps with the idea of selling photographs to the tourists.

Clifton Suspension Bridge, Bristol. Note the health baths on the right.

The Lion Rock, Cheddar

Berry Head, Torquay

The Gorge, Cheddar.

*This is thought to be the
entrance to Gough's Caves.*

✃ A FAMILY ALBUM ✃

'Elizabeth Date Davis from her Grandpa, Myrtle House, Watchet'

The photographs in this volume are all taken from a unique album still in the keeping of James Date's direct descendants, who very kindly gave us the sole opportunity to have their treasured possession digitally captured and reproduced here for everyone to see. Previously knowing almost nothing about James Date, it was quite by a stroke of luck that I first came to set eyes on the album early in 2001, after a passing conversation with Nick Cotton in the Cotton gallery in Swain Street, Watchet. A man with a fascination for the history of his (and James Date's) home town, Nick sent me off on the trail of what turned out to be a wonderful find. Once in touch with the keepers of the album, I was again fortunate in discovering that they had known my own grandparents for many years; so it was that I was warmly welcomed into their home to see hundreds of beautiful Victorian images of the area in which I have also had the pleasure to grow up and work. Over a year later, we were given the family's permission to proceed with the present volume. Our warmest thanks are extended to them for this privilege.

When we contacted renowned photographic historian Professor John Hannavy about the project he arranged to make the long journey down to the West Country to view the album for himself and was not disappointed by what he saw, as testified by his fascinating introduction, 'James Date and Photography'.

The dedication to Elizabeth Date Davis with which the album begins is one of a tantalisingly small handful of clues which we have about its provenance. In all there are nearly 500 images included in the album, which amounts to but a fraction of Date's photographic output. Whilst many of them are very similar, it was felt that a reproduction of the complete album, showing the photographs faithfully laid out in their original order and complete with Date's own, if brief (and occasionally incorrect), captions would be of great interest to many. Unfortunately none of the photographs is assigned a date in the album, and they do not run in chronological order. They are reproduced at just under 85 per cent of their original size.

It is hoped that readers will find the collection as exciting as have the very many people who have helped with this project; our grateful thanks are extended to each and every one of the individuals who has helped with the identification of images.

Naomi Cudmore (Editor)
Halsgrove House, 2002

Watchet

Watchet

Watchet

Watchet

Watchet

Watchet

Watchet

Watchet

Watchet

Watchet

Watchet

Watchet

Watchet

Watchet

Watchet

Watchet

Watchet

Watchet

Watchet

Watchet

Watchet

Watchet

Watchet

Watchet

Watchet

Watchet

Watchet

Watchet

Watchet

Watchet

Watchet

Watchet

Watchet

Watchet

Watchet

Watchet

Watchet

Watchet

Watchet

Watchet

Watchet

Watchet

Watchet

Watchet

Watchet

Watchet

Watchet

Blue Anchor

Watchet

Watchet

Watchet

Watchet

Watchet

Watchet

Watchet

Watchet

Watchet

Watchet

Watchet

Watchet

Dunster

Dunster

Dunster

Dunster

Dunster

Dunster

Dunster

Dunster

Dunster

Dunster

Dunster

Dunster

Dunster

Dunster

Dunster

Dunster

Dunster

Dunster

Dunster

Dunster

Dunster

Dunster

Dunster

Dunster

Dunster

Dunster

Dunster

Dunster

Dunster

Dunster

Dunster

Dunster

Dunster

Dunster

Dunster

Dunster

Dunster

Dunster

Dunster

Dunster

Dunster

Dunster

Family

St Decumans

Lydeard St Lawrence

115

Minehead

Minehead

Minehead

Minehead

Minehead

Minehead

Minehead

Minehead

Minehead

Minehead

Minehead

Minehead

Minehead

Minehead

Minehead

Minehead

Minehead

Minehead

Minehead

Minehead

Minehead

Culbone Church

Porlock Weir

Porlock

Minehead

Berry Head

Berry Head

Williton

St Audries

Berry Head

Cleeve Abbey

Cleeve Abbey

Cleeve Abbey

Cleeve Abbey

Cleeve Abbey

Cleeve Abbey

Cleeve Abbey

Cleeve Abbey

Cleeve Abbey

Cleeve Abbey

Cleeve Abbey

Cleeve Abbey

Cleeve Abbey

Cleeve Abbey

Cleeve Abbey

St Audries

St Audries

St Audries

St Audries

St Audries

St Audries

St Audries

St Audries

St Audries

St Audries

St Audries

St Audries

St Audries

St Audries

St Audries

Nettlecombe

Nettlecombe

Nettlecombe

Nettlecombe

Nettlecombe

Nettlecombe [HUISH BARTON]

Nettlecombe

Nettlecombe

Nettlecombe

Nettlecombe

Nettlecombe

Nettlecombe

Monksilver - Rectory

Williton

Nettlecombe

St Decumans

St Decumans

St Decumans

Watchet

St Decumans

Watchet

Watchet

St Decumans

Watchet

Watchet

Watchet

Watchet

Ilfracombe

Ilfracombe

Ilfracombe

Brendon

Brendon

Brendon

Brendon

Brendon

Brendon

Cheddar

Brendon

Naked Boy

Brendon

Cheddar

Cheddar

Cheddar

Cheddar

Cheddar

Williton

Williton

Williton

Williton

Williton

Williton

Williton - Orchard Wyndham

Williton

Williton

Cheddar

Nettlecombe

Williton

St Audries

Nettlecombe

St Audries

Weacombe

Weacombe

Weacombe

Weacombe

Weacombe

Weacombe

Weacombe

Bristol

Weacombe

Old Cleeve

Old Cleeve

Old Cleeve

Old Cleeve

Carhampton

Carhampton

Cleeve

Brendon

St Decumans

Watchet

Watchet

Watchet

Watchet

St Audries

Watchet

Watchet

Watchet

Watchet

St Decumans

Watchet

Watchet

Dunster

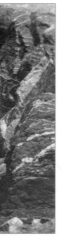

Watchet

Watchet

Watchet

Watchet

Watchet

Watchet

Watchet

Watchet

Watchet

Watchet

Watchet

Watchet

Watchet

Watchet

Watchet

Watchet

Watchet

Watchet

Watchet

Watchet

Watchet

Watchet

Watchet

Watchet

Brendon

Watchet

Watchet

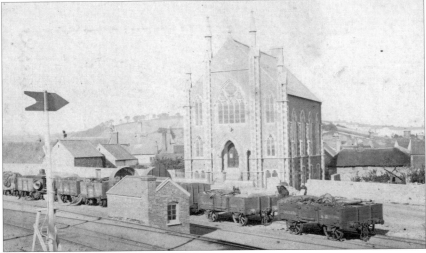

Watchet

Watchet

Watchet

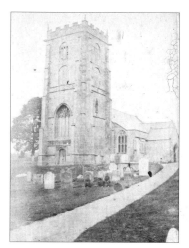

Old Cleeve

Watchet

Watchet

St Decumans

Monksilver

Watchet

Watchet

Watchet

Watchet

Watchet

Watchet

Watchet

Watchet

Watchet

Watchet

Watchet

Watchet

Watchet

Blue Anchor

Blue Anchor

Blue Anchor

Blue Anchor

Blue Anchor

Blue Anchor

Abbey

Blue Anchor

Abbey

Abbey

Abbey

Abbey

Minehead

Minehead

Minehead

Minehead

Minehead

Minehead

Minehead

Minehead

Minehead

Minehead

Minehead

Minehead

139

Minehead

Dunster

Dunster

Minehead

Minehead

Dunster

Dunster

Dunster

Dunster

Dunster

Dunster

Dunster

141

Dunster

Dunster

Dunster

Dunster

Dunster

Dunster

Dunster

Dunster

Dunster

Dunster

Dunster

Dunster

143

Dunster

Dunster

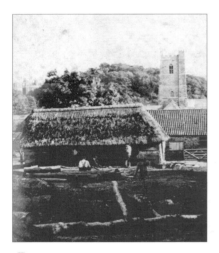

Dunster

Dunster

Dunster

Dunster

144

St Audries

St Audries

St Audries

St Audries

St Audries

St Audries

Brendon

Brendon

Nettlecombe

Combrow

Combrow

Brendon

Nettlecombe

Combrow

Combrow

Combrow

Monksilver

Brendon

Porlock Weir

Porlock Weir

Porlock Weir

Porlock Weir

Porlock Weir

Porlock Weir [LYNMOUTH]

Culbone

Culbone

Lynmouth

Culbone

Abbey

Lynmouth

Watchet

Lynmouth

Monksilver

Lynmouth

Minehead

Valley of the Rocks

Watchet

Valley of the Rocks

Ilfracombe

Watchet

Watchet

Ilfracombe

St Audries

Cheddar

Watchet

Cheddar

Watchet

Cheddar

Dunster

Minehead

Minehead

Dunster

Dunster

Minehead

Dunster

Dunster

Dunster

Dunster

Dunster

Dunster

154

Watchet

Cheddar

Cheddar

Williton

St Audries

Cheddar

Watchet

Watchet

Watchet

Watchet

Watchet

Watchet

Watchet

Watchet

Watchet

Watchet

Watchet

Watchet

Watchet

Watchet

Watchet

Watchet

Watchet

Watchet

Williton

Williton

Alcombe

Lydeard St Lawrence

Watchet

Alcombe

Watchet

Watchet

Old Cleeve

Brendon

Watchet

Watchet

Watchet

Watchet

Williton

Nettlecombe

St Audries

St Audries

St Audries

St Audries

Nettlecombe

Nettlecombe

Watchet

St Audries

Nettlecombe

Watchet

♀ [ST AUDRIES]

Dunster

♀ [GOYLE]

St Audries

Wife?

James Date

Family

Family

Family

Family

Family

Family

Family

Wife

Family

Family

Family

Family

Family

Family